THE FOUR HATS
OF LEADERSHIP

BE WHO YOUR PEOPLE NEED YOU TO BE

THE FOUR HATS
OF LEADERSHIP

BE WHO YOUR PEOPLE NEED YOU TO BE

DRAKE E. TAYLOR

New Insights Press

Published by New Insights Press, Los Angeles, CA
Editorial direction and editing: Rick Benzel
Copyediting: Julie Simpson
Cover and book design: Josep Book Designs

Printed in the United States of America
ISBN: 978-0-9995801-9-6 (print)
ISBN: 978-1-7338411-0-8 (eBook)
Library of Congress Control Number: 2019936822

This book is dedicated to all of my
mentors throughout my life:

To all the military men and women I've served with.

To my family – my parents, my sister and
brother, my son and daughter.

To my friend Kae and to my loving girlfriend, Alessandra,
who really helped buckle me down to finish this.

Without these incredible people,
you wouldn't be reading this.

CONTENTS

THE SELF-CARE HAT

WEARING ALL FOUR HATS

LEADERSHIP LIBRARY

PREFACE

Thank you for choosing to read my book. I hope you will gain new insights from it and that it challenges you to develop your leadership style. My goal is to create a quick and easy read for leaders on the go and those who need a concise, non-scholarly, practical guide to a new way of thinking about leadership. I am not one to throw around big words nor to cite a lot of statistics. I prefer to speak straight-forwardly and honestly about how to become a great leader, something I have learned about through my education and experience in the Air Force.

Over the years I have had many opportunities to lead. I have also been placed in positions where I was expected to follow and others to lead. I learned just as much, if not more, about leadership from those times as a follower as when I was leading.

There are many leadership positions that you may step into in your career. You may have direct or indirect responsi-bility over people, money, processes, business units, or entire organizations. Whether you are leading your peers through a specific challenge at work or heading up a team of 50 to assault an enemy stronghold, how you lead people depends on your frame of mind about your role as a leader. That's what this book seeks to focus on, using the simple metaphor that leaders wear four types of hats — a farmer's hat, a drill instructor's hat, a psychologist's hat, and a self-care hat. Each of these hats serves a different purpose — and you need all four to be the type of leader your people need you to be.

How I got my start

Leadership is a very simple but frightening word. To have it thrust or thrown upon your shoulders is especially difficult when you think you are not ready. I never thought I was ready to be a leader, but somehow I became one. This is my story.

I am currently a Captain in the United States Air Force, as a Security Forces Officer. Officers like myself are responsible for a multitude of tasks within the Air Force, many involving security, as well as managing people and equipment. The Air Force can have the most sophisticated piece of equipment on the planet yet if there is no one to manage it, it's useless. My "careerfield" (an Air Force term) is focused on military base security, law enforcement, and being part of a Quick Reaction Force while we are in deployed locations. We safeguard America's nuclear weapons and have a section called Executive Aircraft Security, charged with coordinating aircraft security for our nation's top leaders when transiting the globe, including the Secretary of Defense (SECDEF), the First Lady (FLOTUS), the Vice President (VPOTUS), and others.

I became a leader in the Air Force probably due to my background going all the way back to my teenage years. My first instance of leading others began in Ohio where I was class president during my junior and senior years of high school. My class had more than 500 kids in it and we were among the largest high schools in Ohio. Back then, before you were able to become class president or leader of the student body, you were required to attend the Ohio Association of Student Councils (OASC). This was (and still is) a two-week summer camp that taught us leadership skills. This was the start of my thinking that I wanted to be a leader.

Being junior and senior class president helped me learn how to create a vision for others to follow. I was also co-chair of Fundraising and Student Activities groups, and these roles helped me learn how to organize, go out into the community, ask for financial assistance, and put together large teams of kids to execute dances, car washes, fundraising drives, and so on. I experienced bumps along the way, as any leader does, but they provided me with lessons to learn from.

My next step into leadership was not straightforward, though. After graduating high school in the summer of 2004, I began college at the University of Cincinnati but dropped out during my second quarter. I had been working at the Hamilton County Justice Center (the largest jail in the state) and I continued to do so. There I learned a lot about people and how you cannot trust a book by its cover. I met numerous people who seemed honest, but their crimes told a different story.

I joined the Air Force in 2005 and was sent to basic training. If you have not served in the military, here's how it works. You are assigned to a unit, which in the Air Force is called a squadron. The squadron is then divided into groups known as "flights," typically 30-70 people. These are led by a Training Instructor (TI), which in the other military branches is called a Drill Instructor (DI).

I remember my recruiter telling me not to stand out, but

rather to blend in so the DI would not pick me for a job I didn't want, such as Dorm Chief (DC). In Air Force basic training, the Dorm Chief is equivalent to a platoon leader in other branches. This is the most stressful job you can have in the military, outside of being in combat, because everything your flight fails to do is deemed your fault. DIs are in charge of leading their entire flight of recruits from all walks of life to try to get them to become a team and they choose a DC to help them lead the flight. I didn't want that job, so I paid close attention to the recruiter's instructions and wore a gray polo shirt and jeans so as to blend in when I reported for duty my first day.

Then I recall hearing, "Hey you!" The DI came straight over to me and said, "Yes, you! You look kind of smart. Get in front and be one of my *element* leaders." The term "element" meant I would be in charge of everyone behind me in line. That assignment went on for a week, then after our first physical training test, I was chosen to be the flight's Dorm Chief.

Despite my hesitation, I recall feeling excited at first because I was chosen to lead. Then it quickly sank in: I had no idea what I was doing. I was just some 20-year-old kid who had been high school class president and worked at a jail before joining the military. WTF did I know about being a leader? This was different.

It was definitely the most challenging leadership task I had up to that point in my life. I still draw upon those experiences to help me lead to this very day. And frankly, it is actually a leadership position in which I believe I failed miserably. I went in with a mindset that everyone joined the military because they were deeply patriotic, wanted to serve their country, and would give their very last breath to defend it. I thought everyone believed in the oath we took before getting to basic training and again upon graduation: "I do solemnly swear to support and defend the Constitution of the United States of America against all enemies, foreign and domestic, that I will bear true faith and allegiance to the same, that I will obey the orders of the President of the United States and the officers appointed over me, according to regulations and the Uniform Code of Military Justice." But the people in my flight came from various walks of life. It was there that I learned firsthand how everyone is motivated differently.

It was apparent that many other flights had problems, though not exactly the same as mine. While other flights had many men who were not the sharpest tacks in the box, shall we say, my flight was too smart. This caused a lot of issues. We played a mental game of chicken, as many guys were hell bent on making their own rules. They were what are often called "mavericks." You can only succeed in the military when you act as a team, not as single individuals, each man for himself.

When I saw my flight didn't want to come together, I began trying to survive myself. This totally shattered my world because of the naïve idea I had about what basic training should be. But this soon changed. I remember speaking with the Senior Master Sergeant in my squadron. He called me into his office and told me how I had more responsibility than 85% of other men entering the military will ever have, enlisted and officer alike. I was leading a group of 50+ people, when most others would never lead more than 2-4 their entire career. At that point, I sat down and thought, "Wow;

he's absolutely right." I was shaken out of my self-survival mode and returned with conviction to encourage my flight to operate as a unit.

From there, I led a summer internship as a "two striper," meaning I now had two stripes on my arm. In that role, I learned to give specific, measurable goals to my crew, drawing on my past experiences and using lessons I learned from when I had failed in the past.

I eventually left the military and went into the reserves so I could go back to college. During that time, I joined the Air Force ROTC. At one point, I was allowed to join my peers in Maxwell, Alabama for 28 days for officer basic training. Here I held multiple leadership positions from flight commander to group vice commander.

After completion of my field work, I returned to the ROTC detachment and was given my own flight of 32 people. In this position, I generated tests and quizzes outside of the usual ones to help my people associate better with military life. I then held two additional leadership positions in the detachment, as wing IG and drill and ceremonies cadet officer.

One day, I was asked to give a speech on leadership and what it meant to me to. I thought back to everything I had accomplished up to this point in my life. I dissected each leader I had and examined their good points and their bad ones, and gave my speech on leadership. I entitled it *The Three Hats a Leader Must Wear*, which turned into Four Hats later on. That speech became the foundation of this book.

I say this jokingly, but please don't go out and buy four different hats. Being in the military for 12 years, I have learned to spell out my instructions. The hats are a metaphor for how you need to think.

I use the Four Hats approach all the time in my work and even in my personal life. It works well in a military career, but I know it equally applies to leadership in any field. Whether one is talking about military security, selling insurance, or making widgets, there is a mission that must be completed, threats detected and deterred, and teams of people to lead forward. It's imperative that you know how well your men and women are prepared for their jobs, where their heads are at, and what you can do to help them ease their mind, so they are relaxed and focused on their work. Leadership is much more than barking orders to tell people what to do and how to do it. Anyone can do that. It takes time and thoughtfulness to be a leader. There are many great leaders out there, and I suggest that none of them got to where they are without knowing how to guide and inspire their followers.

One of my favorite quotes is:

> *"Regard your soldiers as your children, and they will follow you into the deepest valleys; look on them as your own beloved sons and daughters, and they will stand by you even until death. – Sun Tzu.*

The Four Hats approach asks you to examine each situation and lead from a 360-degree perspective to get the very best out of your people as well as yourself. Part of this approach is equally knowing how to follow. Too many leadership books teach you how to lead but not how to follow.

You can't have one without the other. We all lead someone, but we also follow someone, from the President of the United States to the citizens within this nation. Leadership is a continuous circle; understanding that and using the four hats is paramount to success in either role you assume.

There is no particular order to wear the four hats in to be a leader. Each hat signifies a trait that a leader must possess to be effective in the given moment. You adjust your hat to what the moment calls for.

Why we need great leadership

Before you continue reading about the first hat, let me add a final word. I wrote this book because I believe great leadership is a fundamental and necessary part of a thriving society. So much is changing in our world that we need many new leaders to help us find the right vision and guide us into the future.

Not everyone has an interest in being a leader, nor perhaps the raw talent to be one. Yes, there are some people whom you meet and are just automatically drawn to. You want to follow them wherever they go, even into the depths of hell itself. People like that are rare; they exude that much confidence from your first impression of meeting them. But in today's society, it is safe to say that most people must first prove themselves before others will follow them even down the hall to the copy machine.

If you want to become a leader, and don't believe you have the raw talent, don't hold yourself back. You can learn how to be a great leader using this book. You can aspire to improve your skills and develop the traits that help you attract people to follow you. I have learned that many people don't know they are leaders until they are put in a position or given an opportunity to lead. It's a question of whether or not you will rise to the challenge when called upon.

Dwight D Eisenhower said:

> *I think that there is something to the expression "born to lead." But there are many people who have the potential for leadership, just as there are probably many people born with the potential to be great artists that never have the opportunity or the training for the full development of their talents. I think leadership is a product of native ability plus environment. By environment, I mean training and the opportunity to exercise leadership.*

To become a leader, one must not shy away from leadership opportunities. One must seek them out, not for the sake of power but for the sake of the greater good of society.

I hope you enjoy this book and will use it to become part of the next generation of great leaders that the world needs.

Best regards,
Drake

THE FARMER'S HAT

"Farming looks mighty easy when your plow is a pencil and you're a thousand miles from the corn field."
Dwight D. Eisenhower

You're probably wondering why a leader needs a farmer's hat? How does one get leadership out of a farmer?

Frankly, the farmer's hat is one of the most important hats you will wear as a leader. It is probably the hat you will wear most often.

Think about the farmer. He or she is dedicated to getting up early in the morning and spending all day out in the field. He has various plots of land for which he must select the right seeds to plant. He has to tend to the crops for many months, carefully cultivating and nourishing them, all the while monitoring their growth. When they are ripe and mature, he has to decide the right moment to harvest them.

As you can see, the farmer is actually a very apt metaphor for some of the major roles a leader takes on.

THE 6 STAGES OF FARMING AND LEADERSHIP

et me discuss with you in detail how a farmer is similar to a leader by examining what I call the six stages of farming: crop selection, land & environment preparation, seed selection & sowing, irrigating & fertilizing, monitoring the growth, and harvesting the crop. You will readily see how these stages encompass the very things that leaders must know how to do.

Crop selection

The first thing a farmer must do is to select the types of crops he or she wants to grow. In business terms, this is the equivalent of knowing what projects you have to work on.

Of course, when leading, you aren't always able to choose your projects as they may be assigned to you. In the military, as in business, you sometimes inherit a wide array of projects with a varied mix of deadlines and complexities. This is like a farmer inheriting a bunch of fields already planted. When this occurs, your job is to take stock of the crops (projects) and make sure you understand how they were planted (initiated) and what expectations for their growth have been set by those before you. Depending on when the project began and how well it has been led so far, you may need to make adjustments, just as a farmer does sometimes when a field is not producing as intended. Sometimes crops must be plowed under rather than waste any more resources on them.

Land & environment preparation

This phase involves creating a great environment for your seeds (your people) to grow in. You have to inspect and cultivate your soil to get it ready for planting. What is the best environment to allow the majority of your seeds to flourish? What can you do to prepare that soil for the plants you want to grow? What tools have you invested in and which will you use? Is there enough rain (money)? Will they have adequate protection from all the elements: heat, cold, rain and storms (other people, conflicts, politics, and saboteurs who don't like the project)? Will they be able to weather anything that is thrown at them? These questions are both literal and figurative depending on your projects and the work environment you are in.

There are many things you can do in order to be successful when trying to create the right environment for your team. For example, you can do some preparation in writing, such as creating a guide book or project plans to help direct your people along the way. Use this to share with your teams your vision of the job and how you intend to lead them. Your project plans can explain the rules of the job and the values you live by. They are like the straight line furrows in the field where the seeds are to be planted. You can prepare these furrows so you have a suitable environment that allows your people to thrive, flourish, and grow into productive members of your organization — or even into leaders themselves.

4

Depending on your work setting, you can reinforce your project plans by putting up inspirational posters or sayings on the walls of the offices. Or you can offer a reading shelf with books from great writers and/or poets and invite everyone to borrow the books. You can also use biographies and memoirs of famous and well-respected leaders.

Another idea is to create a name or title for your group so they feel like a team rather than a bunch of individuals. A team name helps people feel connected and recognize that they depend on each other to win. You'd be surprised by how just something as small as this idea will enhance their buy-in to the goals and ambitions you have for the group.

In the military, each squadron has its own distinct mascot and saying that fosters pride in its organization. If your organization doesn't have a name, create one. I guarantee it will go over well. However, do this with caution. Choose a name that won't offend anyone. You might invite members to help with the process of naming themselves; it will have more meaning for them if they were part of the decision-making process. When you name something, you take ownership of it, so you don't want it to fail!

In most of the flights I've led, I always started the day or the shift with an interesting quote that I read to everyone. I've always been taught that when you know more you do more, and when you think more, you learn more. My goal is to pass this approach on to my fellow airmen as part of preparing the land (their minds) for the growing season. Even if you are leading a group of older workers, I believe we are never too old to learn something new.

I also start many group meetings by explaining what my expectations are for the coming days. This sets the stage for how I want the work to occur; it's like establishing the environment and the climate I desire. Without setting up the environment, you allow weeds to take root and little animals to nest on your plot of land. Then, when you begin to plant your crop, these weeds and critters will be a challenge to get rid of.

Seed selection & sowing

The seeds are the people you need to put into place to handle each project. In seed selection and sowing, your goal is to choose the specific person or people you want to assign to each project or team. You first must decide how many individuals you want or need for each project. Can a small number of seeds turn into the harvest you seek to obtain? Or do you need many seeds? Will you devote more time to one, two, or three plants than you do to the rest of the crop? Or will you treat the entire crop the same and not select particular ones?

When placing each person into their specific position, it's key that you have looked at his or her record and experiences. Have they been in this type of position before or not? Will you need to tend to them more than others because you know what the seed is made of but want to give it a little more nourishment than others? Wearing your farmer's hat reminds you that you must maintain a knowledge base of all your seeds — your followers or subordinates — and care for them so they grow strong and produce the harvest you want.

If you are just joining an organization, you usually do not have the luxury to pick seeds. They have already been selected and planted long before your arrival. However, this gives you the opportunity to inspect the people along their stage of growth and see the potential each one has. Be careful here, as you reap what you sow. So take time to inspect and figure out what seeds you already have and if they have been properly planted.

Beware of this: many seeds may appear to be the same, however you will always have a few that don't match the others. That is where you must examine the seeds closely to have a deep baseline assessment of them so you will know where each one might need to be planted. You consciously need to understand their skill set and how they add to the overall team.

Usually leaders try to plant the right person into the job where they are confident their skills match the others on the team and everyone will get along. However, I also believe that sometimes you need to weigh the strengths and weaknesses of each person and put people together who have complementary skill sets. This helps your long-range planning and building of a great team.

Consider this example: What if you had a team in need of a drastic overhaul and you know you have to put in two new people. You have three people in mind whom you think could fit in. As you further examine the individuals, two of them are very similar, with the same strengths and weaknesses. You don't know the other candidate very well, but the person seems to have an opposite set of strengths and weaknesses.

The question: Do you choose the two similar ones because they have the same qualities and would flow better together? Or do you try to place two people with opposite skill sets together? If you chose the latter answer, you may benefit more than the former choice.

My view as a leader is that it is better to strengthen each person's weaknesses to make them stronger overall. If you continue to develop only someone's strengths, you will have failed that individual because their knowledge and skill sets are too narrow, and they will be suited to only one task in the future. They will not maximize their growth and their value to your organization.

Irrigating & fertilizing your crop

Irrigating and fertilizing refer to ensuring you supply your crop with what it needs to grow and mature into the outcome you want to obtain. In farming terms, these two actions help you remember that you may need to replenish lost nutrients to ensure that this year's plants have the food they need to flourish. From time to time, every project needs more support, resources, sunshine (motivation), and some fertilizer (fairy dust like a celebration, party, time off, rewards, etc.).

One of the best ways to irrigate and fertilize is to talk to your people. Find out what road blocks they have, what might be missing from their soil (environment), and if they can use more sunshine. Make sure they have all the tools they need to get their jobs done.

For some people, a small amount of irrigation and fertilizer is enough to keep them going. But many others need constant attention and motivation to stay on track. Things happen in life that take their focus away from the project, and this can either keep them stagnant or lose them completely if they aren't being continually nourished.

There are some people who go through life in a zombie-like state. They get so accustomed to being on auto-pilot that you really have to jumpstart their minds to get them back to reality. Sometimes you have people whose educational backgrounds are simply lacking. In my work, many of my flight members joined the Air Force right out of high school or a few years of college and that's all. Some had teachers who spent time on the arts and taught them about the great thinkers of human history, but some had a poor level of education. I try to level the playing field for them.

This is where fertilizing comes in handy. Why not have a weekly or daily watering (meeting) to keep your team motivated and learning on a path to build their capabilities. For instance, at the beginning of each shift, I always start with one or two quotes of the day. I do this to get their minds thinking. I once started a particular formation with this famous quote from Hall of Fame football player Emmitt Smith: "Your dreams are only your dreams until you write them down, then they become goals." Try that one on your team.

Leadership is a constant cycle. You must continue to cultivate each crop and tend to it. You must water and fertilize it or it will perish. For when you stop watering and fertilizing, the plant stops growing and begins to wither and die.

Sometimes a little fertilizer goes a long way. A few years ago, I had flight members working on New Year's Eve. We could not drink alcohol as we were carrying weapons with live rounds in the course of our daily duties to secure the base. My technical sergeant at the time, J. B., and I were discussing how hard it can be to have to work on a holiday and not be able to spend time with our loved ones to usher in the New Year.

I suggested that we go over to the commissary on base and get enough bottles of non-alcoholic sparkling cider for everyone to make a toast at midnight. We rushed over to the store before it closed, drove to every post and handed out the bottles and cups and told everyone that if our radios were clear at midnight, we would do a collective countdown and celebrate as a family. Finally, in the wee hours of the morning, when everyone went home, they told us how no one had ever done that before for them and it meant the world to them that their supervisors cared. They didn't feel forgotten. Doing small things like that is the fertilizer that teams need.

In another instance, I did something special for some members of my team in ROTC. Many officers in training are not on scholarship and have to hold jobs on top of attending ROTC classes. When life events come up — birthdays, deaths in the family, etc. — you as the leader need to notice signs of change in your people and see if anyone needs special attention. I had a member whose mother became ill and another whose grandparents passed away. I noticed slight changes in their behavior because I knew them well. They hadn't even told me about their personal situations, but I arranged for them to reschedule their tests and I created take-home class material so they could travel to be with their loved ones during these times of crisis.

The point is: Take care of your people, even if they don't ask. It has been my experience that many people simply won't tell you what is really going on in their mind until you ask them two or three times. Many think they should not inconvenience their team, but if you show you care, you can help them. I will discuss this in greater detail in the chapter on the psychologist hat.

This is often especially true with young people. They may give you a different answer than what you want out of fear of rocking the boat. So you may need to dig deep and ask lots of questions to fathom out what is going on inside their mind. Trying to find the right balance of information/help/support can be tough but consider it an important part of your job as leader.

Monitoring the growth

This stage is critical because you cannot assume all is well, just as a farmer cannot go on vacation in the middle of growing season. You have to take time to check on how your crop is growing, and even take measurements to validate the growth. Monitoring your crop is how you check to see the progress made and where the crops are along the continuum of being ready to harvest.

Dutch author, consultant and motivational speaker Alexander Den Heijer says, "When a flower doesn't bloom, you fix the environment in which it grows, not the flower." In this context, you may need to water and fertilize more, giving your people far more time, resources, and tools. You need to fix their environment rather than blaming them.

But sometimes you may need to make a larger adjustment by moving seeds or plants. Some plants might need to be uprooted if they are not doing well in a particular patch of dirt. You may need to give a plant more attention or replace it in a more suitable place where it can thrive.

Monitoring your crop is your insurance policy against failure.

Harvesting the crop

Harvesting is the final stage when farmers get to reap the rewards of their hard work. First, they must inspect the final crop before sending it to the store to be sold. This can involve checking each plant to see if it passes the quality test. If it does, the farmer knows it can be sold and someone will benefit from it. If not, the plant may not be ready to harvest and should stay in the ground longer.

In business, this is the stage when leaders reap the rewards of their projects, both in terms of the results produced (a product or service, monetary results, etc.) and taking pride in the work of their teams. Effectively, for business leaders it is a double harvest – the projects and the people. Of course, you hope both have come out fine and you will have a tremendous harvest. If yes, it is the right time to look back and take stock of what worked as well as a time to celebrate. If not, it is the time to understand what went wrong and to celebrate the small wins in the larger loss.

For leaders in business, taking stock of the past months or year is often done in a debriefing or strategy review session to discuss the profits from your product or service, and in the form of performance reviews for your people. Let's talk just about the people for now, though.

You want to go over with each team member what they have accomplished, how they grew, what they learned, and what they believe they can do better. Some of your team members might have excelled or succeeded very well and you wonder if you should reward or promote them. Ask yourself questions like: Have they mastered everything you taught them? Have their results exceeded your expectations? Are they ready for new responsibilities? Answering yes to such questions is your indication that they are ready to be harvested.

Other people under your leadership may have struggled to grow and their results are disappointing. As much as it feels sad to take action, sometimes you need to give up on a plant and admit that you cannot keep growing it. It does not fit your soil or the environment. In that case, you cannot harvest these people but must let them go.

A plant that you think is worth saving may need a little more attention and care. People will tend to give you what you put into them. That's why it's important to make sure you have tried your best to help each one grow. In their performance review, give them honest feedback, both positive and negative. However, be prepared for some people to be standoffish or defensive. Some folks do not like feedback or cannot take constructive criticism. They perceive it as you pointing out their flaws, which makes them uncomfortable. Those who are receptive, however, are plants you want to continue growing. They recognize that your feedback is an opportunity for them to learn and grow.

The harvesting stage is an important one, not just for this year, but for future years to come. It is when you can take stock of how the past year went and make plans for the coming growing season.

✻   ✻   ✻

As you can see, comparing some elements of leadership to "wearing a farmer's hat" is a pretty good metaphor for how you need to think about your people. They are the seeds that you must plant, nourish, and harvest to succeed in your own role as a leader.

THE DRILL INSTRUCTOR'S HAT

"You don't lead by hitting people over the head — that's assault, not leadership."

Dwight D. Eisenhower

We all know from movies and TV, or if you have actually served in the military, that there is no other figure or career that exemplifies leadership more forcefully than that of the Drill Instructor (DI). Just the image of the DI is about as serious as you can get. When people think about a DI, they immediately see a spotless uniform with hard creases that can cut a man's finger, shoes so shiny you can see your face in them, and the most distinctive symbol – the DI's hat.

In the military, the DI ensures everyone respects the importance of duty, honor, service to country, the importance of teamwork, and above all else, "attention to detail." Armed with their voice to bark out commands and a several other intimidating tools, the DI wears an enforcer hat and commands that everyone must follow his or her directions…no ifs, ands, or buts. It is the most rigorous and strict form of leadership, which some organizations no longer believe in. But in my view, sometimes wearing a DI hat is the only way things get done.

Many people's interaction with the military is when a family member graduates from Basic Military Training and they get to meet the famous Drill Instructor. If you have ever been to such a graduation or watched the movie *Full Metal Jacket*, you know that graduates invariably say that the DI is a person they greatly appreciated. Though their methods of leadership are despised and loathed by anyone under their command, when people follow the DI's instructions and complete their training, most always end up with profound respect for the DI.

There are many reasons that the military has drill instructors rather than just teachers. When you arrive at basic training, in the eyes of the military, you know nothing. You may think you do, but you don't. Recruits in the various branches are people who come from different walks of life, with many races, religions, social economic classes, political affiliations, and reasons why they enlisted. With such variety of individuals and the goal of turning them into serious, well-trained fighting machines, there must be a single conduit that tears everyone down at the same time and allows them to rebuild themselves back up as a team. Most people think that drill instructors enjoy being mean. But it's all a role they play to get the best out of every individual and push each person past their limits to achieve things they may have never known they were capable of.

THE DI'S FORM OF LEADERSHIP

Feared by most, hated by some, and respected by all, drill instructors use a variety of tools to perform their leadership function. Let me go through these before we look at how and when you might use the DI hat in your leadership role. Not every quality below is what you will adopt, but let me first walk you through what I consider to be a military DI's tools.

A barking voice, a cutting stare, and in-your-face commands

Doesn't matter whether it's the Army, Air Force, Navy, Marines, or Coast Guard, if you've served in any of these branches of military, you know the DI uses his/her voice to demand action. It is loud, crisp, clear....and commonly perceived as yelling and screaming at you. It is usually harsh and mean-spirited and feels like gasoline is being poured over you. If you were a civilian in business and your boss behaved like a DI, that thunderous voice would be cause for their being fired.

But yelling is very useful in the military and it is what Drill instructors are best known for. As captured in the beginning of *Full Metal Jacket*, R. Lee Ermey's character yells and screams at his marine recruits. A DI knows that, for whatever reason, some people only respond to someone who is in their face and yelling at them when trying to accomplish a task or when being corrected for a mistake — and they take advantage of this truth. In fact, they tend to treat everyone the same way, even those who are paying attention and willing to listen. Everyone gets yelled at.

The second infamous tool in this category is the DI stare…by which I mean a cold, searing, direct look that cuts through you like a knife. When the DI stares at you, it feels like they are a monster about to eat you and spit you out like a bad-tasting piece of meat. It's worse than any mother's or father's stare when you were a child and did something wrong. At least with your parents, you knew they loved you, but with the DI, there is no love.

The third tool in this category is the DI's tendency to be in your face. When they are yelling at you, they step up to within inches of your face and talk to your mouth and eyeballs. Their breath usually ain't pretty, and their proximity to you is more uncomfortable than having a zombie standing next to you. You can feel their presence crawling all over your skin and you just want to run away…but you cannot.

Detail driven, disciplined, & chasing perfection

Nothing escapes the DI's attention. They are totally detail driven, seeking out the cancers — the bad soldiers – that might infect their beloved branch. One untucked corner of your shirt, a loose bedsheet, a drop of mud on your shoe, a crooked tie, the stubble of a 5 o'clock shadow on your face — nothing escapes the eagle eye of the DI. Worse, nothing can be incorrect, out of order, or done wrong. No mistakes are allowed. The DI's motto is like what famed football coach Lou Holtz said: "In the successful organization, no detail is too small to escape close attention."

Thanks to their keen regard for detail, the DI strives for a constant state of discipline. Again, football coach Lou Holtz summed it right up: "Winners embrace hard work. They love the discipline of it, the trade-off they're making to win. Losers, on the other hand, see it as punishment. And that's the difference."

The DI thinks that without discipline and someone holding you accountable, you are destined to fail. They seek to instill a sense of pride and ownership, as they want you to be self-sufficient and be able to handle yourself in any situation. Discipline is required for everything you do in the military. It does not allow sloughing off, waking up late, overeating, drooping your shoulders when you walk, or not cleaning up after yourself. Discipline is how you win wars and how you survive when others don't.

The upshot of being detail driven and disciplined is that DIs seek perfection. They personally strive for — and demand that their personnel strive for — 100% perfection. Soldiers can argue that the goals and standards established by this God are impossible to achieve, but the DI will shout back at you, "Drop and gimme 50," meaning get down on the floor and do 50 pushups. The DI is effectively saying, "Hey, perfection is possible if you do what I tell you to do." If you get up after your 50 and argue again, the DI will just tell you to drop again and do another 50. You can't win.

Motivates by rewards and punishment

There are many ways DIs make their trainees learn. One is that they offer rewards for those who do things right the first time or who win competitions. People love rewards — it is built into the human psyche. Who doesn't want to get something special as a prize for doing what your parents/ teacher/DI tells you to do? For example, a DI might reward someone with an extra hour to write a letter to one's family, or extra time in the shower, or even just being able to buy something from the vending machine. For the really lucky, the reward might be a surprise visit to a military history museum.

On the other side of the equation, the DI never refrains from punishing those who don't listen. The penalties are not always aimed at the lone culprit who failed, as the DI could punish the entire group because the group allowed the behavior to happen or did not assist in helping the person see the error of his/her ways.

And yelling is just step 1 of punishment; if you don't improve after some yelling, step 2 is forcing you to do something extra or nasty, like cleaning toilets, sweeping up after others, or a 10-mile run. Step 3 of punishment may be taking something away from you, like free time or a weekend visit home or making you miss out on an activity — one that you would rather be doing than trying to repeat something everyone else has mastered or managed to get right the first time.

Tough love

The ultimate goal of a military DI is to turn individual soldiers into in-shape, disciplined, tough fighting men and women who are team players. The foundation of what they do is what my mother used to call "tough love." In my definition, tough love is the intersection of instilling fear and inspiring confidence. When leading people in the military especially, particularly large groups of people, one often has to try to accomplish both of these goals – making people fear the consequences of failing and yet instilling confidence in them at the same time so they believe they can succeed.

✳   ✳   ✳

These are the qualities of a military DI. They are hard-nosed, no-bullshit, hardened, insensitive bastards, but by the end of training with your DI, you cannot imagine how you lived life in any other way. You now understand the reasoning behind the DI's thinking and his or her tactics of making people do what he or she says. You may even recognize that the tough love lessons you learned from the DI have built a new foundation for the rest of your life. Everything you learned from the DI, including everything you despised at first, will change your life as you go to war or continue your career in the military.

HOW YOU CAN USE THE DI HAT IN YOUR LEADERSHIP ROLE

learly, many of the tools in the DI hat are not appropriate in the business world, especially in today's climate of sensitivity about bullying, political correctness, and other trends. Training and leadership in the military does not serve the same purpose as training and leadership in the corporate world. Leaders in both worlds can draw on the strengths from each other as there are similarities, but the differences must be kept clear. You cannot act like a true DI in the business world.

However, there are some elements of the DI hat that I suggest can be useful in any leadership role. You may not wear the DI hat very often, but it cannot be forgotten. There are times in the business world when you need to instill discipline, be detail driven, ask people for perfection, and even operate on a tough love basis.

Few people really like to play the disciplinary role as a leader, and especially today, everyone wants to be liked and be known as a fun person. The corporate world appears to be changing, offering lots of rewards and seldom imposing punishment. Who wants conflict when you can motivate people with extra time off, bonuses, free lunches, trips to the movies and museums, etc.?

No one should want to rest solely upon the DI hat as

THE FOUR HATS OF LEADERSHIP

their leadership style. Using this as your sole leadership method leads to a dictatorship mentality. This is one I assume no one wants — to rule with an iron fist. However, there are times when you have to be stern, serious, and downright strict with others to convey the gravity of the situation. If you are not able to put on the DI hat when it is needed, you run the risk of being taken advantage of and not respected.

Here are some adaptations for how you can wear the DI hat in a civilian business-like way:

Yelling. Yelling is almost always off limits in the business world. In the military, it's an everyday occurrence. But even if there are people in your company who yell, it's not a good policy to allow it. Who wants an office full of yellers?

However, you may absolutely need to yell to correct a serious infraction of the rules or a breach of safety. If you have to yell, only hold the full volume for a few seconds, getting directly to the issue at hand. If you keep your voice elevated for too long, you run the risk of losing the person's attention altogether. When reprimanding someone, ensure that you use your voice, but then modulate it back down and end on an even tone. Unless their mistake is grave, keep it brief and to the point. Then walk away, cool down, and ask them to think about what you said.

Do not use yelling as a form of intimidation and control. If you do, you will find that the people under you will simply seek out new employment and let others know you are an angry person. Unless people have been in military training, they just won't understand your yelling. Studies show that yelling is counterproductive and yelling at children is just as harmful as physical abuse. Using vulgar names and unconstructive criticism can have the most adverse effect. That's why using a loud voice must be done in a manner that is constructive and very brief.

If you do yell at someone, be sure to use constructive words, not personal attacks like calling the person stupid. Keep your anger aimed at the specific act of infraction. Once the fires have cooled, you can approach the person from a calm but stern manner and engage him or her specifically to discuss why the yelling was necessary in that single instance. Let the individual explain to you why he or she did what they did. If they are able to explain it calmly, then switch to your psychologist hat (discussed in the next chapter) and explain to them what was wrong about their actions. Always ensure that you give the person a way forward, such as commending them for trying to make a good decision if their explanation made any sense to you.

Using a special stern voice. This is like the voice your mother or father would talk to you in when in public and they didn't want to yell but to ensure you knew they meant business. This demanding voice is reserved for special situations. When you use it, think of the occasion as requiring your DI hat. For example, you may need to sit someone down and lecture them if they are doing something incorrectly and jeopardizing time, resources, or other people. Or you may need to approach your upper management to advocate for your team to demand things they are not getting. These are times when you need to speak in a stern tone of voice…not yelling, but louder and more aggressive than your normal voice. Be careful, though. This hat must be used with great caution. You must use it only when necessary and you feel nothing else will work.

Physical proximity. You can use your posture and physical proximity to express sternness. Nothing is more intimidating than getting in someone's personal space and inviting confrontation. I'm not saying that you should get right up into someone's face as a military DI does, but you might step closer to someone than you usually do if you have to reprimand them.

Asking people to buy into high quality work, if not perfection. A crucial part of any good leader's goals is ensuring that your people do their best work possible. Perfectionism is a wonderful goal to have, although it can also become a monkey on everyone's back and a time waster if carried too far in the real world when getting products out and work is time sensitive. But when you need to do it, don't refrain from wearing your DI hat once in a while to inform people that their work is not up to par and you want them to redo it.

Called an inspection in the military, this is a formal review of your team's work. When you find things wrong, you need to explain why the work is shoddy and get them to buy into your insistence on accepting only the highest quality work. Inspections are dreaded in the military because soldiers fear being held back or sent back a week in their training (known as being recycled). But the DI must check everyone's progress to ensure they are meeting standards and can correctly demonstrate that they are proficient in their tasks. Some of these individuals will be replacing parts and doing mechanical work on jet engines, so people's lives are at risk. Wearing the DI hat allows you to feel confident that your team is performing the best they can.

Surprise, shock, and awe. This is exactly what it sounds like. It is a technique that needs to be used wisely.

Unless you have a profession that dictates you maintain this character a majority of the time, it must be used sparingly. In the military, the term Shock and Awe is a tactic based on the use of overwhelming power and spectacular displays of force to paralyze the enemy's perception of the battlefield. This may be what you must do at times with some of your subordinates, but it needs to be done in a way that inspires and motivates them when there is a major inspection or obstacle they must attack.

The corporate world is organized around routines: 9 to 5 hours, five days a week, lunch hour, meetings, and so on. One idea that you might borrow from the DI playbook is to surprise your team with a different reaction. This can be done when your team is doing a tremendous job, such as surprising them with an especially fantastic reward, or when they are not doing well at their work or loosening up on your standards. In the latter case, your goal is to catch your personnel in a way so they are completely caught off guard and not expecting your response. This often helps when you need to regain control of a situation.

I recall one powerful example of shock and awe from when I was in basic military training. Each one of us received an individual task. This was our own task and ours alone. During one short notice inspection, the DI inspected one trainee's wall locker contents. When the DI opened the drawer, he lost his mind and chucked the drawer across the room. As he did that, he noticed the trainee twitch. He approached him and made him "cage his eyes" (i.e., stare directly in front), then he got up in his face. He was so angry, you could see the veins in his neck throbbing from across the room. He demanded to know why the trainee had just thrown his socks into his locker rather than rolling them up. The trainee began to stammer, being caught off guard. Before he could answer, the DI added, "Did I hurt your feelings," in a very sarcastic manner. He screamed that what he just witnessed was unacceptable and would not be tolerated. Then he turned to the entire flight and told us, "You have one hour to ensure that everything is in inspection order. If not there will be some remedial training," by which he meant push-ups, crunches, wall sits, planks, and any other thing he could think of to make us not want to repeat these mistakes. With that, he left the barracks and the flight got to work on getting all our wall lockers for inspection order —and we all focused on the sock drawer.

This is clearly not the type of action that any sane businessperson would take, but we have all heard stories of bosses who "lost it." So be careful if you decide to implement a shock and awe punishment, lest you get carried away. In some small cases, it can be useful as it gets people to sit up and take notice that something is terribly wrong.

Demonstration. Sometimes to get people to do things that they claim cannot be done (because deep down, they don't want to do the task), you have to show them that it's entirely possible. In this instance, you have to behave like a DI to demonstrate the activity and do it with ease. Effectively, you are embarrassing your team by proving that you can do what they cannot do.

Enforcing discipline. In many elements of life, discipline is a great habit to have. Teaching your teams to have a strong disciplined approach to their work can pay off in many ways. Without discipline, people lose the importance or significance of things. Discipline instills in us a sense of pride and teaches us that certain things must be done a certain way — or not done at all.

Drill instructors use discipline to train individuals to obey rules and codes of behavior, using punishment to correct disobedience. In the military, there are certain rules imposed because they build habits of getting things done right and paying attention to detail. Some things may seem trivial, such as folding a pair of underwear or rolling socks in a certain way, but the reason these rules are followed is to teach discipline. If that soldier becomes an aircraft mechanic, the practice of paying attention to how they fold their underwear can make the difference in ensuring they are disciplined about getting every rivet and bolt in the right place and tightened perfectly. Think of how many accidents have been caused by human error resulting from a lack of discipline.

So if your people are losing their sense of discipline, start reinstating it with small details and work your way up to the big issues. The people you supervise may require as much discipline as that aircraft mechanic.

✳   ✳   ✳

The DI hat, while you may not wear it often, is nevertheless an important and vital hat to keep in your wardrobe. You are unlikely to make any of your personnel drop and give you 50 pushups, nor are you likely to yell into their ear when they screw up, but your leadership may require at least once in a while that you take on the countenance and some of the attributes of the steel-chewing Drill Instructor, who is not to be messed with.

THE PSYCHOLGIST'S HAT

"Leadership is solving problems. The day soldiers stop bringing you their problems is the day you have stopped leading them. They have either lost confidence that you can help them or concluded that you do not care. Either case is a failure of leadership."

Colin Powell

When I was a young airman, around 21 years old, I worked in an office setting. I worked with computers, running base programs. I had been doing this job for a year when I got a new superintendent who was not familiar with the methods we used regarding electronic folders and permissions for sub-folders. I taught him what he needed to know.

A week later, one of the organizations on base had a server crash and they had the communication squadron pull all their data from the last back up. This meant that each folder had to be given a new set of permissions. My superintendent came to me and explained what I had to do. He was very longwinded about it and, being frustrated and young, I got upset. It made no sense that he was explaining to me how to do what I had just explained to him a week before. I guess you could say I blew up at him.

Needless to say, my attitude did not make him happy. He left the office, called my supervisor into his office and told her that I had until 1600 hours to have all the permissions set. If I failed to do this, my annual award package would not be submitted. Needless to say, I was distraught and did not like being threatened. In my view, he was taking a DI approach to manage the situation when it actually needed a far more psychologically insightful and sensitive approach. It wasn't the right hat to wear to handle the situation.

DEEPENING YOUR PSYCHOLOGICAL LEADERSHIP SKILLS

Sometimes leaders need to put on the hat that a psychologist would wear. This hat reminds you that the situation calls for good judgment, an even temperament, exceptional listening skills, and the ability to look deeply at a problem and understand how people feel about it. The psychologist uses his or her voice and calm demeanor to talk to everyone involved in a situation and get to the "heart" of the matter. I use the word "heart" intentionally to signify that your focus is not just on the facts of the situation but equally, or even more so, on the emotions that people are feeling.

The psychologist speaks without judgment or ego. You become fully self-aware, understanding that your own interactions and mannerisms play a role in how people engage with you. Most people are very reserved and won't open up about their problems, and many people even believe that no one cares. You must therefore be open and accepting of others when you wear this hat.

To break through the clutter in the minds of the people you lead, you must engage with them from a neutral standpoint and show your complete willingness to listen to whatever they have to say. Remember: they want to feel that their leader is speaking to them at their level, not coming from a high place and treating them as just another body or number.

The psychologist's role is to help people work through the difficulties life throws at us all. This includes mental disorders, anxiety, depression, relationship problems, substance abuse, parenting, family issues, grief and dying, and more. The goal of wearing this hat is to help people deal with issues that affect them in their lives, especially guiding them through difficult times and helping them seek the assistance they need so that life issues do not affect their work ability long-term.

For most leaders, the usual number of people they supervise at a time is from one to five. Being able to connect with each of them is crucial and goes a long way to being a great leader. Being intuitively in tune with people is a gift, but it can also be learned. This is done by genuine everyday interactions. Begin by taking time to watch how your people think, their mannerisms, sense of humor, and moods. By noticing these qualities, you can develop a keen sense about whether people are having a good day, a great one, or a bad one.

Most people cannot hide how they feel inside; their feelings automatically rise to the surface and are visible in their tone of voice, gestures, word choices, and how they relate to others. So it is your job as a leader using your psychologist hat to understand the people around you. Of course, you will not be able to solve every single problem or challenge that others have but trying your best to relate honestly and forthrightly to others and convey that you understand what they are experiencing can go a long way.

You will come across people from many different walks

of life throughout your time as a leader and you will need to learn how to read them. It's a crucial skill to learn if you want to be an outstanding leader. You have probably heard it said that communication is only 7 percent verbal and 93 percent non-verbal. The non-verbal component is made up of body language (55 percent) and tone of voice (38 percent).

Of course, leading 10, 20, or 100 people is a completely different challenge. Most leaders of large groups cannot possibly be observant of so many people to the level described above. If this is your situation, you need to pay attention to the closest five to seven people around you and ask them to wear their psychologist hat with the people around them. This sharing of responsibility will make for a better and healthier environment.

This is not to say that you shouldn't look after anyone outside of your five or seven people. If you notice something in any of your personnel, take action and notify the person in charge of that individual to check into the situation. In some cases, you may even take the individual aside and get personally involved if the situation calls for your higher-level leadership.

When you wear your psychologist's hat, one thing you have to watch for is giving others the impression that you are flawless. Many subordinates admire their leaders and think of them as perfect beings who don't have any problems. After all, they seem so successful. Some leaders I know even try to maintain an image of themselves as "holier" than others, as if they are the only ones who have psychological smarts.

I suggest that authenticity and honesty will be respected more. Allow others to know that you are human, and that you also have problems in life. Especially if you've been through some of the same issues they are facing, and you can relate to them, others become more confident in confiding in you.

Keep in mind that you need to understand your people so you can know what might be causing any performance decline. Then you can either help them through the problem using your psychologist hat, or you can reassign or reschedule them appropriately. In some cases, you may even be the one who can help save their career or their life.

Building trust and maintaining confidentiality

There is a very simple concept that many leaders get wrong. I've seen it time and time again, especially with new leaders. They get in their heads that once they assume their position, the people who report to them will automatically divulge their deepest secrets and feelings to them; e.g., how they feel about their job, their colleagues, or the entire organization. That is not the case. It is sometimes harder to build relationships when you are in a leadership position. People are aware that things they say can be used against them to either discipline them or get them fired. They are going to be cautious around you because they are not sure if you are there for them or your own career. Some may have been burnt in the past by a leader and are going to be much more careful in confiding in you.

One of the key challenges of leadership is building trust. It doesn't happen automatically. Many leaders fail because of a failure of trust. People may not give you their trust due to what they have already encountered with past leaders in their life. If your reports feel you are not genuine with them, you will not get their loyalty nor their buy-in to the team.

Especially important, always treat anything people tell you with the utmost confidence. Do not reveal to anyone what any of your personnel tell you about their private troubles or inner feelings unless you have a legal obligation to do so or their consent. No one wants to have their secrets revealed to others; they do not want to be laughed at or talked about.

Making the right assessment

To be able to fully help your subordinates when they have problems, you must correctly assess their situation. One tendency when you wear the psychologist hat is to arrive at a conclusion too quickly and make the wrong judgment about what the problem is. Hear the person out entirely so you can grasp all aspects of the situation. This allows you to ask further questions so you are better able to evaluate and assess what issues they might want to tackle and in what order that might be beneficial to them.

For example, let's say you have an employee, John, who is constantly turning in his weekly reports late. They are due on Monday morning, yet he never turns them in before Tuesday by close of business. So you give John a pep talk and say he must do better. He says he is "busy" on Monday mornings with other work but he will try. He looks unusually stressed, but you accept his promise without asking further questions or taking 15 minutes to talk with him.

What you failed to learn, however, is the full story. By noticing but not asking about John's stress, you do not actually know his entire situation, i.e., that his child has a disability who requires special attention so he takes on that role as soon as he enters the door. Also his wife was recently laid off her work a few weeks ago and now he is the sole provider. He no longer has help from his mother because she moved into an assisted living home after a stroke a few months back.

By only seeing one small sign and not acting on it, you knew that something has changed but you do not understand why. Your deadline has now added to his stress, by reminding him of what he already knows and feels bad about, rather than helping him become more productive by finding what stresses there are in his life.

It's also important to NEVER assume what someone's living situation or financial status is. You have to dig deep when there are problems and seek to get a 360-degree view of the situation before making your assessment. It's important to build the relationship so you can assess what a person needs to do in certain areas of their lives.

In the clinical field of psychology, the first step a psychologist has to take is get to know the patient. What brings them in to see you? How did they grow up? Are they married, single, or in another type of relationship? What is their educational background? What are their hobbies? What causes them stress or grief? How do they manage their stress? These are all important to a psychologist because it begins to paint a picture of the person and allows you to see what makes an individual tick. What someone holds to be important in their life gives the therapist clues as to how to relate to what the person is feeling at a particular moment.

As a leader, you should ask your subordinates these

questions as well. It will give you better insight into how to manage and lead them. It will also let them know you care more than just about the mission or task at hand. This is a very important element in having people feel part of a team, not just a cog in a wheel. You will get more out of your personnel if you get to know them. You will be better able to lead them and know what motivates them and when they might need help and support from you.

Your manager's office is not the only place to talk to your people. A café, a walk around the building, or a match on the tennis court can become your "psychologist's office" where your "client" can begin a talk session. Making sure your subordinates or teammates feel at ease and relaxed is important, so if feasible allow them to choose the place or offer suggestions.

I once had a soldier in my group, we'll call him Mark, who was having marital problems. We were at the smoke-pit taking a break and I asked him how he was doing. I had noticed he was not being his usual self. He answered that he was "doing fine." But I could tell by his tone of voice that something was not right; his voice gave away that he was hiding his real feelings.

I asked to talk to him privately after the others left. I told him that I could hear something was wrong and asked if he'd like to discuss it. "I understand your wanting to keep stuff private if you prefer," I added. "Just know that if you want to talk, I'm here."

He stared at me for a few seconds; I could see he was reading my facial expressions and processing my caring tone of voice. He then opened up and told me about his marital problems. Having been through marriage problems of my own, I could relate to his frustration, sadness, anger, sudden mood swings, and confusion about what to do. We talked for a good 40 minutes, discussing options that might help him salvage his marriage.

Knowing that he needed time to sift through the marital situation, I assigned him a local task rather than sending him off on a mission away from home. Ultimately his marriage ended, but he was much better able to deal with the residue of his marriage. I gave him a smaller role in the section rather than put more work on his shoulders or demand a higher performance from him when he was not capable of doing that. Taking the time to ask and dig deeper not only allowed me to help him by giving him a more relaxed position in an already demanding job; it also gave him more time to work through what he needed to with his wife.

Understanding the inner emotions and private life of your people is vital to good leadership. Whether it's allowing someone to attend their child's rehearsal or giving them time off for a family member's birthday, or just to go home early one night and make dinner for their spouse — these are leadership gifts that go a lot further than one may think.

THE PSYCHOLOGY OF GOAL SETTING

One of the key elements of leadership is helping set goals for each person on your team. In my view, there's an element to this goal setting that requires you to wear your psychologist's hat. It's like asking your patients, "What do you want to get out of therapy?"

This is where the psychologist's hat is particularly important. As we all know, not everyone has the same background or experiences. Each person comes into their job with different goals, ambitions, and dreams. Some may want to rise in the corporate hierarchy, while others just want to do their job and get paid. Still others are confused and don't know what they want out of their job or even out of life itself. This is where you want to help try to steer them and have them think deeper.

I suggest that you sit down with each of your team members and ask them about their dreams and what they want out of life. This will help you gauge their goals and understand how to reward them for jobs well done. It will also give both of you a timeline for where they need to be at certain points to help them achieve their dreams. Without asking for this information, you cannot assume that you know their goals. If you do, you won't get buy-in from them, nor will you get their best work.

Studies show that people typically work better when

they have a goal in mind. Knowing this, you can work with them to come up with a plan to help them. This collaboration will cement the fact that you care about them as individuals. People will typically work harder and longer if they feel they are being looked over and cared about. Helping them achieve their full potential and giving them something more than just a work schedule to accomplish your goal or mission will give you better work productivity.

Stay away from being controlling. When trying to empower people, it's contradictory if you tell them everything they have to do. If you've been in leadership positions or been to seminars, I'm sure you've heard of the acronym SMART, created by George Doran, Arthur Miller, and James Cunningham. It first appeared in 1981 in an issue of *Management Review*. This model has helped leaders everywhere. It sets criteria for what you expect yourself or any person you supervise to accomplish in their goals. SMART stands for: Specific, Measurable, Achievable, Realistic, and Time-bound.

- **Specific.** Give specific goals, give them the parameters for the task you want completed.
- **Measurable.** When giving them a task ensure they are able to measure their progress in clear terms.
- **Achievable.** Don't assign a task you know they obviously cannot complete given the budget and timetable. This not only sets them up for failure but will give you a reputation that you have unrealistic goals and people will shy away from working with or for you.

- **Realistic**. Ensure that the task is humanly possible to achieve. Don't exaggerate how easy it is or pretend it can be done in a certain way when you know it is not true.
- **Time-bound.** Give a specific time for completion: e.g., 1:30 pm on Thursday.

This is a bit like a treatment plan that a psychologist sets up for a patient. To help determine the way the treatment needs to be structured, goals are set up with certain dates and deadlines. There can be some fluid goals, but typically the more solidified they are, the better.

There are four stages to goal setting:

1. **Develop a relationship.** You must develop a relationship with your subordinates, both formal and informal based on mutual trust and respect.
2. **Make an informed assessment.** This is a process in which you listen objectively to what your subordinate desires. You need to ask fact-based questions and get specifics to help you in the examination of your subordinate or team member.
3. **Establish mutually agreed upon goals and objectives.** Now is when you can give them advice to the best of your ability. Supervisors often have more life experience because of their age, and this allows them to draw on a greater wealth of knowledge to help steer younger people in the right direction on their own path to solving whatever issue they might have. People are always wanting to better themselves and look to others from whom they can learn.

4. **Develop and implement the plan.** This is when you help tailor the plan and generate connections and ideas that could help them reach their goals. You might assign a timeline as S.M.A.R.T suggests.

This entire process can be time consuming and not everyone needs it. But for those who do, it is an important part of being their leader.

PHASES OF CHANGE REACTIONS YOU WILL OFTEN ENCOUNTER

When people go through change, it is said that they go through five stages: Denial, Anger, Bargaining, Depression, and Acceptance. This model is based on the five stages of grief that was developed by Elisabeth Kübler-Ross regarding how people react to the death of a loved one. But I believe this model also works for anyone undergoing any type of significant change in their life. They may go through these phases in sequence, or they may jump ahead, then come back to an earlier phase, finally to finish the entire process months later. It is important to be aware of these phases when you notice one of your subordinates going through a personal change or ordeal. Let me comment on each phase.

Denial. People will often deny that they have an issue or problem they cannot solve, until that problem spirals out of control and starts to affect them in every area of their life. Sometimes they might not even realize that there is an issue until confronted with it. In my time as a leader, I've seen sudden outbursts of anger on one hand, and complete withdrawal on the other hand. These may be tipoffs that someone is in denial of a deep-seated problem.

Anger. Once a problem is recognized, people will often react by becoming very angry at others. They are effectively taking out their resistance to change on people around them. They will find fault with what others do rather than accept responsibility for their own mistakes or accept the reality of a situation that they do not want.

Bargaining. In this phase, people may sometimes reach out and try to negotiate a different deal. They almost seem to be no longer resisting, but they are effectively still doing so because they cannot accept the change that is occurring as they try to barter for a better one.

Depression. When people finally understand that change is inevitable, they often enter into a period of depression. They lose energy and hardly want to do anything. It is difficult to motivate them. You may have no choice but to wait for them to arrive at the fifth phase.

Acceptance. What is amazing about humans is that they nearly always come to accept change and adapt to it. They often even come to recognize the change as a better way to live than their previous life.

Be aware of these five phases if you notice anyone in your team undergoing substantive changes in their life.

WHEN YOU NEED TO DO INTERVENTIONS OR TERMINATIONS

There will be times when you need to invite someone into your office to discuss a bad behavior or work ethic issue. These are pivotal moments and must be taken seriously. These are especially moments when you need to wear your psychologist's hat. You will need to discuss sensitive issues with tact, aplomb, and insight. You need to ask questions, listen, and probe to get to the bottom of a behavior problem or issue that has been brought to your attention.

As stated above, don't jump to conclusions too quickly. Look at the issue as if it is an onion, and peel away the layers one by one to learn what is truly at the core of the misbehavior. There may be times when there is a good reason you can accept someone's poor performance or behavior. Or you might discover that nothing can defend the person's actions and some type of reprimand and/or punishment is necessary according to your organization's rules.

In the worst circumstances, you may need to end the relationship with the person and your organization. This can be the most difficult task you face. In today's world, there are increasing legal guidelines for how to terminate people that you must be familiar with to protect yourself and your company. Terminations go beyond the scope of this chapter, but for now, just keep in mind that these events are critical to be conducted properly. We've all heard about too many times when people are terminated and then turn around and commit workplace violence.

At the end, just like a psychologist, you are there to help your people or team get through whatever it is they are facing, not just for them but also for the organization as a whole.

YOU STILL NEED TO GET THE JOB DONE

Knowing your team and being able to relate to them allows you to truly understand the depth of your talent pool. So wearing the psychologist hat from time to time is just as important as the other two hats I've discussed so far. The psychologist's hat allows you to better understand your people in order to build them into the workforce you want.

Be careful though: if you are constantly wearing this hat, you run the risk of focusing too much on people and their problems, and not enough on the mission or job that still has to get done. So keep in mind that you still need to wear your farmer's and DI's hat, too. Your people may love you, yet are you able to fulfill the roles and responsibilities you were hired to fulfill?

This is where many leaders go wrong, mistaking leadership for being nice to everyone in an effort to make them productive. In the military, we have a saying: "Mission first, people always." Many leaders do not truly understand this motto, and some insist this philosophy is downright wrong, insisting "people must come first because they are the ones who accomplish the mission." I understand that perspective. However, from the point of view of the military, and perhaps in the business world as well, without the mission, there would be no need for people. The principle behind this motto is to remind you that, while people always count, you must accomplish your mission.

There will be times where being a leader sucks! It can make you feel lousy if you have to tell your people they must stay late or have to come in over a weekend when they have family commitments. A bad leader will order people to do such extra work without even thinking about the impact it might have on them. But a good leader will be transparent about it and plan the extra work ahead of time. He or she would notify people weeks ahead or at least during the week that extra work time may be required.

It is important that you do not lose focus regarding what is "mission critical" for your job. People and their families do count, yet there is also a job to get done and it is your responsibility as an effective leader to have a plan so that the work gets carried out.

So don't forget that being an effective leader involves both knowing your people and ensuring that you monitor how things are going. When things are going great, congratulate yourself. But when someone is not doing well or sloughing off or appears depressed, you have to address it by putting on your psychologist hat to find out what his or her inner feelings are. Use your connection to your people to support them so they don't affect everyone's performance or make the entire project or task come to a halt.

THE SELF-CARE HAT

"Caring for your body, mind, and spirit is your greatest and grandest responsibility. It's about listening to the needs of your soul and then honoring them."
– Kristi Ling

This is probably the most important, yet most overlooked of the four hats. I admit that even I have forgotten to use this hat from time to time.

As leaders, we often try to provide a strong image of ourselves that our subordinates can look up to. We work too hard, too many hours, and run ourselves into the ground at times. We take our responsibilities so seriously that we do anything and everything to accomplish our tasks and ACHIEVE mission completion.

We take it to heart that our people expect us to have everything together and never falter. However, we are just like everyone else. We too make mistakes and we need to admit them. When we are afraid to show our subordinates that we have made mistakes, they will feel as if they, too, have to be perfect — and that adds further to our stress. Leading a team whose drive is to be perfect (based on a false premise that their leader is perfect) wears us down. We are never at ease because we feel we have to always be perfect.

WHY NO SELF-CARE IS A
SELF-DEFEATING PROPOSITION

Trying to maintain this false image opens us up to a major problem: We forget to take care of ourselves, as we devote our time to taking care of our projects and our people. In doing this, we risk harming ourselves. It took me years to realize that work will always be there and that I cannot run myself into the ground. I must be able to adequately take care of myself if I expect to take care of others.

I'll tell you a personal story about when I just kept going and didn't take a break. I was working nights at an Air Force base stateside where my leadership role was very demanding. I was working between 50-60 hours per week. I also had a supervisor who insisted on having our weekly meetings at 1:00 pm, just when I would be in the middle of sleep from working my night shift. I was exhausted and eager to get home. I asked several times to change the meeting time to 8:00 am, so it could coincide with getting off my shift and not in the middle of my sleep, but he refused.

To make matters worse, I was married, and we had a child. I dearly wanted to spend time with my family, of course. So after these 1- to-2-hour meetings, which would coincide with my child being released from school, I would have to pick her up, then meet my wife at the gym for our workout. I therefore flipped my sleep habits from a day schedule to a night schedule on weekends so I could spend time with them.

My flight sergeant and I totaled up the amount of sleep we got during the week after work hours, spending time with the family, exercise, and other responsibilities. Not to our surprise, it was only a mere 23-27 hours for the entire week; that's about only three to four hours per night, though none of it was a continuous eight hours except on our Sunday day off.

I kept up this pace for months, trying my best to maintain it and not complain. But in the end, it took a huge toll on me. In the span of five months operating at this level, I had two car accidents, fortunately minor fender benders. For the first, my brain was so slow that I backed into a car in a parking garage. For the second, I let my foot off the brake while heading into work for one of those midday meetings. In another incident (though it was not an accident), I was heading home and swerved over two lanes of traffic and nearly missed hitting an ambulance pulling out of a turnaround as it responded to a call. Another time, I literally pulled into my own parking space at my apartment, turned off the car, and fell asleep sitting in it. My wife finally came out and woke me up as she was leaving for work.

The straw that did it for me occurred one Saturday morning when I had gotten home from work at 7 am. I was awoken at 9 am by my wife to go to the gym as we usually did together. Walking down the hallway, I felt a very sharp pain in my chest near my heart that dropped me to one knee. It was sharp enough to make my eyes water. I told my wife I couldn't continue at this pace. I went back to bed, but that was it. No further pains. But I recognized that I had nearly killed other people and almost myself as well. I decided I would not die from this stress and I needed to take a stronger stance with my boss. I needed him to wear the psychologist hat for once.

I finally woke up to reality and decided I could not continue living like this. I had seen myself as a superman who could do anything, but I finally had to admit I was human and needed to place limits on myself. If I didn't take care of myself, who would? If I kicked the bucket, who would take care of my family? Thinking about these questions led me to a drastic change of heart. I had to pay attention to myself. I also finally got a new supervisor who changed the timing of the meetings.

What self-care means for you

You might be asking yourself, "What is self-care for me? How do I even go about improving how I can care for myself?" Here's my take on what you need to do.

We sometimes get so focused on helping others and taking care of them that when it comes to ourselves, we are lost. So I always say, look inside and figure out what makes you happy. Answering this question will require you to be completely honest with yourself. You have to get beyond the quip that many leaders hide behind: "It's work that makes me happy." You simply cannot work all the time; if you do, you are just fooling yourself. Be careful: the stress and toll it takes on your body will catch up with you.

Try to identify some things that you enjoy doing, then go out and make time to do them. Do you enjoy travel? Dancing? Theater? Music concerts? Going to the library or bookstores? Playing sports? Spending time at the gym? Playing cards? Building models? Painting? Sculpture? Think of all the activities you could do and focus on the ones your heart calls out for you to try. If you're having difficulty thinking of activities, check out the list below.

- Cycling
- Running
- Rollerblading
- Fishing
- Hiking
- Painting
- Playing or learning a musical instrument
- Learning a second language
- Kite flying
- Building a model structure (airplane, boat, car, etc.)
- Golfing
- Sailing
- Flying
- Real estate investing
- Reading
- Visiting museums and art galleries

This list does not represent all there is to do in life, but it's a start to get you thinking about the many options you have. Any activity that relaxes you and frees your mind is what to put on your list. Avoid anything that might put pressure on you, such as an activity that makes you feel competitive with others. That just creates stress rather than relieving it.

Avoid activities such as watching TV all day (which is

nothing but an escape), or that involve spending time on a computer for long periods. Watch out for competitive games that get your blood pressure up if you can't just enjoy the game for what it is. Many games just add to your stress, especially if you do poorly or play them in a public room like a lobby where people often end up bickering. If you can remain calm and don't get upset, then go ahead and play video games to your heart's content. But watch out for technology tools that just drain your time and energy. The goal is to find things to do that take you outside into nature or that put you in the company of other people who are not involved with your work.

If nothing strikes your fancy or you simply cannot choose among too many things, I suggest that you simply do one of these things at least one day per week: take a drive to a place that you've never been; go for a hike in a park where you can be alone with your thoughts; or listen to a great album of music that invigorates and energizes you. Use this time to let your mind forget everything about the work world and just enjoy nature and the sights around you. Meditate, listening to your breath and emptying your mind of every detail about work. Seek to purify yourself of all your stresses.

Mental health is not only good for you but for also your family and other loved ones. Your health affects them, even if you don't notice it. When I grew up, my mother was one of the most professional people I had ever seen, completely devoted to her work — and she still is. However, the frustrations she kept inside from her day at work got taken out on our family. I don't mean she abused my father or us children. Yet you could always tell when she had a bad day at work; it was better to stay out of her path because something very trivial could push her over the edge. So we learned not to bother her when we could tell that she had a bad day at work. By no means did this make her a bad person; it simply recognizes that she was under stress and needed to find healthy ways to cope with it. I learned a lesson from her about this that has stayed with me till this day.

My father was a quiet person. He taught at the University of Cincinnati and worked as the director of a halfway house helping to rehabilitate sex offenders and drug users. Even if he had frustrations, he couldn't voice them aloud due to the nature of his work. He had learned not to expose his children to that side of humanity at our young ages.

When I was married and started my family, I resolved to be more like my father. Being involved in Law Enforcement and Security in the Air Force, I faced many types of threats. The job was ever changing; one day could be vastly different from another. It was stressful, but I learned that whatever issues I had at work could not and would not affect my family.

Each evening, as I drove home, I chose to leave all my worries at work. If I was not able to calm down on the drive home from work, I would take five or ten minutes just to sit in the car in my driveway before I entered the house listening to feel-good songs that made me happy. In that time, I gathered my thoughts and figured out what I had to do to "clear my mind." That way, when I entered the house, I would not take my stresses and frustrations out on my innocent family who had nothing to do with the causes of my problems. That's doesn't mean you can't talk about your problems with your spouse or roommate to help get guidance or vent but make sure it's in a constructive manner.

Your life goals count, too

Just as we might push our subordinates to reach for and achieve their highest dreams and goals, we must not forget about ours or put them off for long. Granted, stuff happens, and you may need to refocus. Your priorities may change over time, due to your leadership experience.

However, it doesn't mean that you are not free to set goals for yourself. If you have a goal you want to reach for, it helps if you maintain enthusiasm and excitement about it, even when you are helping others achieve their goals. Always remember that your subordinates are not going to take care of you or ask how you're doing, other than as a formality. Your team comes to you to solve their problems, not to help you solve yours.

This is why it helps to develop your own support group among your peers and a group separate from work. Find like-minded people with the same ambition and drive as you. Set up regular lunch dates with them to discuss your ideas, vent about your work situation, and draw on their strengths. Lean on them for advice.

In addition, select one person older than you or someone with more life experience, and ask him or her to be your mentor. In my career, I've always surrounded myself with people who were older than me to seek out advice and guidance because they understood my drive and ambition. I suggest an older person, but sometimes the advice from someone younger than you can be wiser than you think.

Watch out for leeches

Some people in your life are simply toxic to your physical and mental health. They are like leeches, sapping your energy, stamina, confidence, or dreams. They may be co-workers, friends, or family. In fact, sometimes family members are the worst, given that you can feel that blood is thicker than water and you are supposed to listen to them.

If you give them the opportunity, such people will keep you from reaching your full potential. Learning to avoid toxic people is a key element in your self-care. To be healthy and succeed in your life, you must distance yourself from them. If they are constantly negating what you do, you will feel as if they don't want you to bloom and grow into the individual you want to become.

If you identify people who are leeches to your good health, reduce the amount of time you spend with them. You don't need to argue with them or tell them they are toxic to you; that will only further inflame your relationship. You can be gentle about it, such as cutting phone calls short by saying you have important work to do or keeping meetings with them brief and succinct. It's normal for people to lose touch with one another; so having them slowly disappear from your life can occur as if it is unintended.

One caveat that is rarely shared by other leaders is that people will sometimes try to vilify you for their mistakes. They will try to intimidate you and bring you to your knees. Days may be dark but never let people diminish the beautiful light inside you. Hold your head high and don't let the weight of the world weigh you down.

In the end, what matters most is your self-care. Remember to wear your self-care hat once in a while and you won't regret it.

WEARING ALL FOUR HATS

"The most important thing I learned is that soldiers watch what their leaders do. You can give them classes and lecture them forever, but it is your personal example they will follow."

General Colin Powell

The four hats of leadership need to intertwine in your life. Each has its own purpose in helping you lead and guide your people. No single hat should be worn all the time; you can't use one without the others. You will wear different ones more at different times, but that doesn't make any hat less important.

I have learned over the years that you have to wear the different hats for different situations. If a team member's family has problems, it's not time to use the drill instructor hat. It will most likely be counterproductive and cause resentment from the person you used it on. Eventually, they will rebel or lose all faith in you.

I've had supervisors who rule with an iron fist and only wore the DI hat. They would say things like, "You will be here at this time and no later." "You better not laugh and if I hear you laughing, you're fired." They lead by intimidation and fear. Any leader wearing just the DI hat is going to create a volatile, angry workplace where people are not inspired, only kowtowed into working.

I have also had leaders who were so concerned about my well-being and trying to be my friend that *I* had to keep *them* on task to finish things that needed to be completed. And then there were those supervisors who had great potential, yet they never went deep enough to guide us into truly great performance. They failed to wear the psychologist hat, which would have helped them understand our own ambitions and goals.

START WEARING THE HATS TODAY

A s you go through the coming days, weeks, and months, keep this book in mind. Ask yourself: "What hat should I be wearing now?" whenever you find yourself in these situations:

- a conflict is going on among your team members
- someone is not performing up to snuff
- your team gets a new task or assignment
- you are facing a new challenge that you are not familiar with
- you are feeling confused and don't know why
- your team is not performing in the way you expect them to perform
- your organization as a whole is experiencing difficulties
- there are major changes going on in your company
- and many more situations

The more you learn to switch hats and use each of them as it is intended, the better leader you will become.

To end this book, let me tell you two stories that exemplify the value of using these four hats.

Story #1: Leadership is not black / white

I once supervised a Non-Commissioned Officer (NCO — an enlisted member who is a military officer who has not yet earned a commission) whom I felt had a lot of potential. Although she had done something wrong in the past and had lost a stripe, I always had positive interactions with her and was able to see the qualities and strengths she had to become a leader.

One evening, she received a pass to exit the base and mingle with another nation's military members who were partnering with us on our assignment. As always, our base maintained a strict curfew, but unfortunately, she was six minutes late returning home and was, shall we say, a bit tipsy. Just a few weeks prior, the base had issued a notice that anyone who missed curfew would be reprimanded. She argued with the higher ranking officer on the base, who must have been wearing his DI hat that night. He simply wouldn't cut her any slack and wanted to cite her.

I had two choices at that point. I could wear my DI hat, too, or I could wear my psychologist hat. I chose the latter. I had her escorted back to her sleeping quarters and told her we'd deal with the situation in the morning.

The next day, she came to see me, and we discussed the situation. She revealed various details about her background that made me aware that her career was more complex than it seemed on the surface. A previous leader had filed a report on her for something she did after telling her that he had her back. She no longer trusted leadership and always felt someone was out to get her.

In the end, I decided to take a middle road because I

recognized that wearing my psychologist hat was as important as wearing the DI hat. I was obliged to issue her a Letter of Reprimand about arguing with her ranking officer the night before, but I chose not to put the letter in her personnel file, which would have had a long-term effect on her career. Instead it was classified as a Drawer letter, which meant it would not go on her record unless she messed up again. But I needed to place some type of documentation in her file folder in case there were future problems.

My take on this situation was based on my realistic conviction that *everyone* messes up. In my view, there are few incidents that warrant having bureaucratic paperwork become a permanent record that can negatively impact a person's long-term career. I opted to take a direct approach with this individual, discussing in person the behavior change we needed from her, while at the same time, letting her know that she had potential as a leader herself and we expected leadership behavior from her.

Moral of the story: Many leadership situations are not black and white, but grey. When things are cloudy, hard to understand, it usually means that you cannot wear one hat. You may need two or more hats to figure out what to do.

Story #2: Pass the hats onto others

I once had a Non-Commissioned Officer who was as impressive as anyone I had ever met. His skills were exceptional, so we promoted him to a position of leadership (called an NCOIC). He took over a team that had been having serious problems, and we believed that this new leader would be able to shape them up.

This individual got to work trying to improve his new team. But he was like a deer in headlights when he realized all the problems going on. I helped him out a few times, even on something as simple as cleaning out the office he inherited, which was a mess.

But as time went by, we began getting reports from his team that his leadership style was over the top. Rumor was that he yelled at people, called them stupid, or idiots. He told one of his team members, "Thinking isn't what you get paid to do; that's my job."

When this information got back to my superintendent and myself, we were alarmed. We first validated the rumors we heard just to be doubly sure. Then we asked our NCOIC to join us for a talk. The supervisor wanted to remove him from his leadership position, but I disagreed because what I saw was that he lacked mentoring. He was thrown into the position without any tools or training, and it was our job to help him. I argued that we owed it to the Air Force to get the guy up to speed and fulfill the potential that we originally saw in him.

I prevailed and when I met with the fellow, I taught him about the four hats. I explained that he has the DI hat nailed to the "T" to improve the discipline of his team. Any time he saw a safety or regulation infraction, he was entitled to correct it on the spot. But I explained how he also had the psychologist hat down but needed to fine-tune that hat more whenever he needed to better understand the problems his team was having. I explained how I'd seen how he wore the self-care hat to take care of himself and not allow his team's problems to overtake his mental health. He could not take his stress and frustration out on his team members. Finally,

I explained that the hat he needed to master most was the farmer's hat, to grow his crop, and how his team members were seeds to be watered and nurtured. I reinforced that this hat is crucial to achieving synergy and cohesion in a team or organization.

He absorbed my talk with him and thanked me. We began meeting once per week to discuss his work. I also began to send him leadership articles and gave him homework to read. Of course, as you might guess, this fellow went on to become an exceptional leader whom I am proud to know.

Moral of the story: Don't expect a new leader to understand the complexities of leadership without training, guidance, and mentoring. I suggest that the four hats concept can quickly help any new leader struggling to do a good job in a difficult situation.

TRY THE HATS ON FOR SIZE

I hope that you have found this book useful and that it has allowed you to examine the way you lead. Perhaps you now recognize that you have been using only one or two hats, when these others were available to you. Take time to reflect on your leadership "wardrobe" and begin wearing all four hats as you go forward. Pay attention to how your leadership style will open up, allowing you a greater variety of ways to lead your team(s).

Enjoy the four hats. I wish you great success in your leadership career.

LEADERSHIP LIBRARY

"Don't begrudge the time you spend developing, coaching, and helping your people to grow so they can carry on when you're gone. It's one of the best signs of good leadership."
– Bernard Baruc

In this section, you will find a worksheet and great leadership quotes that I have compiled as tools to use when I mentor and guide leaders. Feel free to use them as you wish.

THE SUBORDINATE QUESTIONNAIRE

I created the form below because many people don't know where to start when leading. I believe that a great starting point is to get to know everyone who reports to you. In my view, this shows that you care about them both as an individual and a valuable asset to the team or organization.

If your organization has no rules against such a form, ask your team members to fill it out (or a similar questionnaire that you create yourself). Then read them closely and take time to learn about your people.

Name: _____ Birthday: _____

Family information you want to share:

_____

_____

_____

Hometown: _____

What do you want to do in life?

_____

_____

_____

Why are you here in this organization?

_____

_____

_____

What do you expect from me as your leader?

_____

_____

_____

What are your goals?

Work:

_____

_____

_____

Financial:

_____

_____

_____

Personal:

_____

_____

_____

Physical:

_____

_____

_____

USING INSPIRING LEADERSHIP QUOTES FOR MEETINGS

I often use inspiring quotes to begin lectures and meetings. Sometimes a quote from a famous, respected leader can have a powerful impact. Many people admire great leaders from history and wish to achieve what they have.

Here are some quotes I have compiled over the years to help start you off in building your own collection of quotes. I have a notebook of my favorites that I've collected over the years so at any moment, if I need to speak, I can pull out a quote and steer my speech or meeting towards that. Use these as tools for your meetings. They are a great way to engender conversation and engage people in thinking about the role of leadership in their life.

I suggest you read a quote and share what it means to you before asking others to comment. Put emotion into the discussion so as to give people a feeling for how it moves you. Once you have introduced a quote, let people have a few minutes to let the citation sink in and reflect on it. It is important that you clarify that there are no wrong answers. This encourages a more open and nurturing environment where everyone feels that they can be open and voice their opinion without being ridiculed by others.

Once the discussion is going, use the quote to zero in on how it relates to what it is you and they are doing in the job.

Explain why you chose that quote and what it was meant to do for them.

You will find using these quotes serves two purposes. First, it opens pathways for your people to think about issues they may never have thought about before. People often find it enlightening and a great learning technique. It opens them up to further growth by introducing new ideas to them and getting them think in a different way than they are accustomed. Secondly, it adds to their sense that you care about their opinions and having open dialogue with them.

✻ ✻ ✻

Leadership quotes

"Use your people by allowing everyone to do his job. When a subordinate is free to do his job, he perceives this trust and confidence from his superiors and takes more pride in his job, himself, and the organization's goals and objectives. Delegation of sufficient authority and proper use of subordinates helps develop future leaders. This is a moral responsibility of every commander."

– LTC Stanley Bonta

"During World War I, while inspecting a certain area, General John J. Pershing found a project that was not going well, even though the second lieutenant in charge seemed to have a pretty good plan. General Pershing asked the lieutenant how much pay he received. On hearing the lieutenant's reply of '$141.67 per month, Sir,' General Pershing replied, 'Just remember that you get $1.67 per month for making your plan and issuing the order, and $140.00 for seeing that it is carried out.'"

– GEN Omar Bradley

"The Nation today needs men who think in terms of service to their country and not in terms of their country's debt to them."

– GEN Omar Bradley

"I would caution you always to remember that an essential qualification of a good leader is the ability to recognize, select, and train junior leaders."

– GEN Omar Bradley

"Furthermore, no leader knows it all (although you sometimes find one who seems to think he does!). A leader should encourage the members of his staff to speak up if they think the commander is wrong. He should invite constructive criticism. It is a grave error for the leader to surround himself with a 'yes' staff."

– GEN Omar Bradley

"A person can be born with certain qualities of leadership: good physique, good mental capacity, curiosity, the desire to know. When you go to pick out the best pup in a litter of bird dogs, you pick out the pup even though he is only six weeks old. He is curious, going around looking into things, and that kind of dog usually turns out to be the best dog. But there are qualities one can improve on. A thorough knowledge of your profession is the first requirement of leadership and this certainly has to be acquired. Observing others is important—trying to determine what makes them stand out. That's why I think we can learn a lot by studying past leaders. Studying Lee, other Civil War leaders, Jackson, Lincoln. Trying to see what made them great."

– GEN Omar Bradley

"You owe it to your men to require standards which are for their benefit even though they may not be popular at the moment."

– GEN Bruce Clark

"Rank is given you to enable you to better serve those above and below you. It is not given for you to practice your idiosyncrasies."

– GEN Bruce Clarke

"Regardless of age or grade, soldiers should be treated as mature individuals. They are men engaged in an honorable profession and deserve to be treated as such."

– GEN Bruce Clarke

Self-Care Quotes

"Take time to do what makes your soul happy."

– Unknown

"When we self-regulate well, we are better able to control the trajectory of our emotional lives and resulting actions based on our values and sense of purpose."

– Amy Leigh Mercree

"When the well's dry, we know the worth of water."

– Benjamin Franklin

"Those who think they have not time for bodily exercise will sooner or later have to find time for illness."

– Edward Stanley

"It's good to do uncomfortable things. It's weight training for life."

– Anne Lamott

"Everybody is different, and every body is different."

– Beverly Diehl

"An empty lantern provides no light. Self-care is the fuel that allows your light to shine brightly."

– Unknown

"Almost everything will work again if you unplug it for a few minutes, including you."

– Anne Lamott

"Sometimes the most important thing in a whole day is the rest we take between two deep breaths."

– Etty Hillesum

"Self-compassion is simply giving the same kindness to ourselves that we would give to others."

– Christopher Germer

"When you are compassionate with yourself, you trust in your soul, which you let guide your life. Your soul knows the geography of your destiny better than you do."

– John O'Donohue

"If your compassion does not include yourself, it is incomplete."

– Jack Kornfield

"People who love themselves come across as very loving, generous and kind; they express their self-confidence through humility, forgiveness and inclusiveness."

– Sanaya Roman

"Love yourself enough to set boundaries. Your time and energy are precious. You get to choose how you use it. You teach people how to treat you by deciding what you will and won't accept."

– Anna Taylor

"Learning to love yourself is like learning to walk — essential, life-changing, and the only way to stand tall."

– Vironika Tugaleva

"There's only one corner of the universe you can be certain of improving, and that's your own self."

– Aldous Huxley

"Invent your world. Surround yourself with people, color, sounds, and work that nourish you."

– Susan Ariel Rainbow Kennedy

"How we care for ourselves gives our brain messages that shape our self-worth so we must care for ourselves in every way, every day."

– Sam Owen

"My mother always says people should be able to take care of themselves, even if they're rich and important."

– Frances Hodgson Burnett

"The love and attention you always thought you wanted from someone else, is the love and attention you first need to give to yourself."

– Bryant McGillns

"We need to replace your vicious stress cycle with a vicious cycle of self-care."

– Dr. Sara Gottfried

"Caring for myself is not self-indulgence, it is self-preservation, and that is an act of political warfare."

– Audre Lorde

"I have come to believe that caring for myself is not self-indulgent. Caring for myself is an act of survival."

– Audre Lorde

"It's not selfish to love yourself, take care of yourself, and to make your happiness a priority. It's necessary."

– Mandy Hale

"When I loved myself enough, I began leaving whatever wasn't healthy. This meant people, jobs, my own beliefs and habits – anything that kept me small. My judgement called it disloyal. Now I see it as self-loving."

– Kim McMillen

"Self-discipline is self-caring."

– M. Scott Peck

"Self-care is never selfish, but it may feel that way when you live a frenzied life."

– Arthur P. Ciaramicoli

"Put yourself at the top of your to-do list every single day and the rest will fall into place."

– Unknown

"With every act of self-care your authentic self gets stronger, and the critical, fearful mind gets weaker. Every act of self-care is a powerful declaration: I am on my side, I am on my side, each day I am more and more on my own side."

– Susan Weiss Berry

"One of the best ways you can fight discrimination is by taking good care of yourself. Your survival is not just important; it's an act of revolution."

– DaShanne Stokes

"The only person you shouldn't be able to live without is you."

– Chris McGeown

"Take the time today to love yourself. You deserve it."

– Avina Celeste

"Don't sacrifice yourself too much, because if you sacrifice too much there's nothing else you can give and nobody will care for you."

– Karl Lagerfeld

"Anytime we can listen to true self and give the care it requires, we do it not only for ourselves, but for the many others whose lives we touch."

– Parker J. Palmer

"Self-care is not a waste of time. Self-care makes your use of time more sustainable."

– Jackie Viramontez

"Rest and self-care are so important. When you take time to replenish your spirit, it allows you to serve others from the overflow. You cannot serve from an empty vessel."

– Eleanor Brown

"The perfect man of old looked after himself first before looking to help others."

– Chuang Tzu

"Self-care is the secret ingredient to Soldier care in a recipe that yields many servings of effective leadership."

— Donavan Nelson Butler

"In dealing with those who are undergoing great suffering, if you feel "burnout" setting in, if you feel demoralized and exhausted, it is best, for the sake of everyone, to withdraw and restore yourself. The point is to have a long-term perspective."

— Dalai Lama

ACKNOWLEDGMENTS

I thank my editor and publisher, Rick Benzel, for his guidance on this book and for his great editing. I also thank Julie Simpson for her copyediting and Jose Pepito for his cover and interior design. Together, Rick's team at New Insights Press helped me produce a book I am proud of.

In addition, I am grateful to all the men and women that I've served under and with, who taught me the good and bad of leadership. And finally, I thank my family and friends for supporting me and giving me the strength in this endeavor to finish this dream of mine.

ABOUT THE AUTHOR

Drake Taylor was born and raised in Cincinnati, Ohio where the foundation of his leadership journey began. After graduating high school and taking a small sabbatical from school, he enlisted in the United States Air Force as an Information Manager. He returned to school at the end of his four-year enlistment, attending the University of Cincinnati where he majored in Criminal Justice. There he also obtained his Officer's Commission. While attending the university, he developed his ideas on "the hats of leadership" that became the foundation of this book. Drake is currently a United States Air Force Officer.

His goals in life are to raise the best children he can because that is the true legacy that men and women leave the world. He has had a strong passion for leadership from an early age and wants people to go through life accomplishing their dreams.

You can follow him on Facebook at <u>The Telescope</u> and Instagram "thefourhatsofleadership." You can also contact him at <u>Draketaylor28@gmail.com</u> with your comments and feedback.

If you enjoyed this book, please leave a comment about it on Amazon or at other book review websites you frequent.
Thank you.

Made in the USA
Middletown, DE
15 February 2020